DATE	START	END	TASK, APPOINTMENT, OR CONTACT	✓

DATE	START	END	TASK, APPOINTMENT, OR CONTACT	✓

DATE	START	END	TASK, APPOINTMENT, OR CONTACT	✓

DATE	START	END	TASK, APPOINTMENT, OR CONTACT	✓

DATE	START	END	TASK, APPOINTMENT, OR CONTACT	✓

DATE	START	END	TASK, APPOINTMENT, OR CONTACT	✓

DATE	START	END	TASK, APPOINTMENT, OR CONTACT	✓

DATE	START	END	TASK, APPOINTMENT, OR CONTACT	✓

DATE	START	END	TASK, APPOINTMENT, OR CONTACT	✓

DATE	START	END	TASK, APPOINTMENT, OR CONTACT	✓

DATE	START	END	TASK, APPOINTMENT, OR CONTACT	✓

DATE	START	END	TASK, APPOINTMENT, OR CONTACT	✓

DATE	START	END	TASK, APPOINTMENT, OR CONTACT	✓

DATE	START	END	TASK, APPOINTMENT, OR CONTACT	✓

DATE	START	END	TASK, APPOINTMENT, OR CONTACT	✓

DATE	START	END	TASK, APPOINTMENT, OR CONTACT	✓

DATE	START	END	TASK, APPOINTMENT, OR CONTACT	✓

DATE	START	END	TASK, APPOINTMENT, OR CONTACT	✓

DATE	START	END	TASK, APPOINTMENT, OR CONTACT	✓

DATE	START	END	TASK, APPOINTMENT, OR CONTACT	✓

DATE	START	END	TASK, APPOINTMENT, OR CONTACT	✓

DATE	START	END	TASK, APPOINTMENT, OR CONTACT	✓

DATE	START	END	TASK, APPOINTMENT, OR CONTACT	✓

DATE	START	END	TASK, APPOINTMENT, OR CONTACT	✓

DATE	START	END	TASK, APPOINTMENT, OR CONTACT	✓

DATE	START	END	TASK, APPOINTMENT, OR CONTACT	✓

DATE	START	END	TASK, APPOINTMENT, OR CONTACT	✓

	DATE	START	END	TASK, APPOINTMENT, OR CONTACT	✓

DATE	START	END	TASK, APPOINTMENT, OR CONTACT	✓

DATE	START	END	TASK, APPOINTMENT, OR CONTACT	✓

DATE	START	END	TASK, APPOINTMENT, OR CONTACT	✓

DATE	START	END	TASK, APPOINTMENT, OR CONTACT	✓

DATE	START	END	TASK, APPOINTMENT, OR CONTACT	✓

DATE	START	END	TASK, APPOINTMENT, OR CONTACT	✓

DATE	START	END	TASK, APPOINTMENT, OR CONTACT	✓

DATE	START	END	TASK, APPOINTMENT, OR CONTACT	✓

DATE	START	END	TASK, APPOINTMENT, OR CONTACT	✓

DATE	START	END	TASK, APPOINTMENT, OR CONTACT	✓

DATE	START	END	TASK, APPOINTMENT, OR CONTACT	✓

DATE	START	END	TASK, APPOINTMENT, OR CONTACT	✓

DATE	START	END	TASK, APPOINTMENT, OR CONTACT	✓

DATE	START	END	TASK, APPOINTMENT, OR CONTACT	✓

DATE	START	END	TASK, APPOINTMENT, OR CONTACT	✓

DATE	START	END	TASK, APPOINTMENT, OR CONTACT	✓

DATE	START	END	TASK, APPOINTMENT, OR CONTACT	✓

DATE	START	END	TASK, APPOINTMENT, OR CONTACT	✓

DATE	START	END	TASK, APPOINTMENT, OR CONTACT	✓

DATE	START	END	TASK, APPOINTMENT, OR CONTACT	✓

DATE	START	END	TASK, APPOINTMENT, OR CONTACT	✓

DATE	START	END	TASK, APPOINTMENT, OR CONTACT	✓

DATE	START	END	TASK, APPOINTMENT, OR CONTACT	✓

DATE	START	END	TASK, APPOINTMENT, OR CONTACT	✓

DATE	START	END	TASK, APPOINTMENT, OR CONTACT	✓

DATE	START	END	TASK, APPOINTMENT, OR CONTACT	✓

DATE	START	END	TASK, APPOINTMENT, OR CONTACT	✓

DATE	START	END	TASK, APPOINTMENT, OR CONTACT	✓

DATE	START	END	TASK, APPOINTMENT, OR CONTACT	✓

DATE	START	END	TASK, APPOINTMENT, OR CONTACT	✓

DATE	START	END	TASK, APPOINTMENT, OR CONTACT	✓

DATE	START	END	TASK, APPOINTMENT, OR CONTACT	✓

DATE	START	END	TASK, APPOINTMENT, OR CONTACT	✓

DATE	START	END	TASK, APPOINTMENT, OR CONTACT	✓

DATE	START	END	TASK, APPOINTMENT, OR CONTACT	✓

DATE	START	END	TASK, APPOINTMENT, OR CONTACT	✓

DATE	START	END	TASK, APPOINTMENT, OR CONTACT	✓

DATE	START	END	TASK, APPOINTMENT, OR CONTACT	✓

DATE	START	END	TASK, APPOINTMENT, OR CONTACT	✓

DATE	START	END	TASK, APPOINTMENT, OR CONTACT	✓

DATE	START	END	TASK, APPOINTMENT, OR CONTACT	✓

DATE	START	END	TASK, APPOINTMENT, OR CONTACT	✓

DATE	START	END	TASK, APPOINTMENT, OR CONTACT	✓

DATE	START	END	TASK, APPOINTMENT, OR CONTACT	✓

DATE	START	END	TASK, APPOINTMENT, OR CONTACT	✓

DATE	START	END	TASK, APPOINTMENT, OR CONTACT	✓

DATE	START	END	TASK, APPOINTMENT, OR CONTACT	✓

DATE	START	END	TASK, APPOINTMENT, OR CONTACT	✓

DATE	START	END	TASK, APPOINTMENT, OR CONTACT	✓

DATE	START	END	TASK, APPOINTMENT, OR CONTACT	✓

DATE	START	END	TASK, APPOINTMENT, OR CONTACT	✓

DATE	START	END	TASK, APPOINTMENT, OR CONTACT	✓

DATE	START	END	TASK, APPOINTMENT, OR CONTACT	✓

DATE	START	END	TASK, APPOINTMENT, OR CONTACT	✓

DATE	START	END	TASK, APPOINTMENT, OR CONTACT	✓

DATE	START	END	TASK, APPOINTMENT, OR CONTACT	✓

DATE	START	END	TASK, APPOINTMENT, OR CONTACT	✓

DATE	START	END	TASK, APPOINTMENT, OR CONTACT	✓

DATE	START	END	TASK, APPOINTMENT, OR CONTACT	✓

DATE	START	END	TASK, APPOINTMENT, OR CONTACT	✓

DATE	START	END	TASK, APPOINTMENT, OR CONTACT	✓

DATE	START	END	TASK, APPOINTMENT, OR CONTACT	✓

DATE	START	END	TASK, APPOINTMENT, OR CONTACT	✓

DATE	START	END	TASK, APPOINTMENT, OR CONTACT	✓

DATE	START	END	TASK, APPOINTMENT, OR CONTACT	✓

DATE	START	END	TASK, APPOINTMENT, OR CONTACT	✓

DATE	START	END	TASK, APPOINTMENT, OR CONTACT	✓

DATE	START	END	TASK, APPOINTMENT, OR CONTACT	✓

DATE	START	END	TASK, APPOINTMENT, OR CONTACT	✓

DATE	START	END	TASK, APPOINTMENT, OR CONTACT	✓

DATE	START	END	TASK, APPOINTMENT, OR CONTACT	✓

DATE	START	END	TASK, APPOINTMENT, OR CONTACT	✓

DATE	START	END	TASK, APPOINTMENT, OR CONTACT	✓

DATE	START	END	TASK, APPOINTMENT, OR CONTACT	✓

DATE	START	END	TASK, APPOINTMENT, OR CONTACT	✓

DATE	START	END	TASK, APPOINTMENT, OR CONTACT	✓

DATE	START	END	TASK, APPOINTMENT, OR CONTACT	✓

DATE	START	END	TASK, APPOINTMENT, OR CONTACT	✓

DATE	START	END	TASK, APPOINTMENT, OR CONTACT	✓

DATE	START	END	TASK, APPOINTMENT, OR CONTACT	✓

DATE	START	END	TASK, APPOINTMENT, OR CONTACT	✓

DATE	START	END	TASK, APPOINTMENT, OR CONTACT	✓

	DATE	START	END	TASK, APPOINTMENT, OR CONTACT	✓

	DATE	START	END	TASK, APPOINTMENT, OR CONTACT	✓

DATE	START	END	TASK, APPOINTMENT, OR CONTACT	✓

DATE	START	END	TASK, APPOINTMENT, OR CONTACT	✓

DATE	START	END	TASK, APPOINTMENT, OR CONTACT	✓

DATE	START	END	TASK, APPOINTMENT, OR CONTACT	✓

DATE	START	END	TASK, APPOINTMENT, OR CONTACT	✓

DATE	START	END	TASK, APPOINTMENT, OR CONTACT	✓

DATE	START	END	TASK, APPOINTMENT, OR CONTACT	✓

DATE	START	END	TASK, APPOINTMENT, OR CONTACT	✓

DATE	START	END	TASK, APPOINTMENT, OR CONTACT	✓

www.ingramcontent.com/pod-product-compliance
Lightning Source LLC
Chambersburg PA
CBHW081620100526
44590CB00021B/3532